DATE DUE	
~~JUN 22 2013~~		

I Am Caring

Mary Elizabeth Salzmann

Consulting Editor, Monica Marx, M.A./Reading Specialist

1-04
19.93

Published by SandCastle™, an imprint of ABDO Publishing Company, 4940 Viking Drive, Edina, Minnesota 55435.

Copyright © 2003 by Abdo Consulting Group, Inc. International copyrights reserved in all countries. No part of this book may be reproduced in any form without written permission from the publisher. SandCastle™ is a trademark and logo of ABDO Publishing Company.

Printed in the United States.

Credits
Edited by: Pam Price
Curriculum Coordinator: Nancy Tuminelly
Cover and Interior Design and Production: Mighty Media
Photo Credits: Digital Vistion, Media Focus, PhotoDisc

Library of Congress Cataloging-in-Publication Data

Salzmann, Mary Elizabeth, 1968-
    I am caring / Mary Elizabeth Salzmann.
        p. cm. -- (Building character)
    Includes index.
    Summary: Describes some of the many ways of being a caring person, including showing your family that you love them, spending time with your friends, and sharing.
    ISBN 1 57765 827-2
    1. Caring--Juvenile literature. [1. Caring.] I. Title.

BJ1475 .S25 2002
177'.7--dc21

                                                                            2002066406

SandCastle™ books are created by a professional team of educators, reading specialists, and content developers around five essential components that include phonemic awareness, phonics, vocabulary, text comprehension, and fluency. All books are written, reviewed, and leveled for guided reading, early intervention reading, and Accelerated Reader® programs and designed for use in shared, guided, and independent reading and writing activities to support a balanced approach to literacy instruction.

Let Us Know

After reading the book, SandCastle would like you to tell us your stories about reading. What is your favorite page? Was there something hard that you needed help with? Share the ups and downs of learning to read. We want to hear from you! To get posted on the ABDO Publishing Company Web site, send us email at:

sandcastle@abdopub.com

SandCastle Level: Transitional

Your character is the kind of person you are.

You show your character in the things you say and do.

Caring is part of your character.

I try to be a caring person.

There are many ways to be a caring person.

Caring means showing your family that you love them.

I am giving my daddy a big hug.

Caring means writing to people who live far away.

We are writing letters to our grandma.

Caring means doing nice things.

I help my little sister see how much she has grown.

Caring means spending time with your friends.

We are telling each other funny jokes.

Caring means helping someone feel better.

I hug my friend to help her feel better.

Caring means sharing with other people.

I am sharing my ice cream.

Caring means being kind to animals.

I hold my kitten gently.

I feed her every day.

What do you do to be caring?

Index

Glossary

animals any living creatures that can breathe and move about

day a 24-hour period, from midnight to midnight

family a group of people related to one another

ice cream a frozen dessert made from milk, sugar, and other flavors

jokes funny stories you tell people to make them laugh

kitten a baby cat

letters messages you write and send to someone

About SandCastle™

A professional team of educators, reading specialists, and content developers created the SandCastle™ series to support young readers as they develop reading skills and strategies and increase their general knowledge. The SandCastle™ series has four levels that correspond to early literacy development in young children. The levels are provided to help teachers and parents select the appropriate books for young readers.

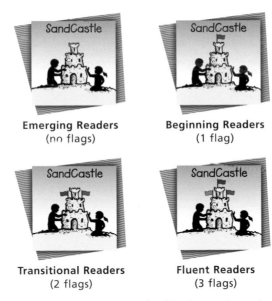

Emerging Readers
(no flags)

Beginning Readers
(1 flag)

Transitional Readers
(2 flags)

Fluent Readers
(3 flags)

These levels are meant only as a guide. All levels are subject to change.

ABDO
Publishing Company

To see a complete list of SandCastle™ books and other nonfiction titles from ABDO Publishing Company, visit **www.abdopub.com** or contact us at:

4940 Viking Drive, Edina, Minnesota 55435 • 1-800-800-1312 • fax: 1-952-831-1632